USBORNE

CAN WE REALLY HELP THE PLANET?

Yes we can!

written by **Katie Daynes**
illustrated by **Róisín Hahessy**
designed by **Helen Lee**

Our planet is a **wonderful** place to live...

...and we want to protect it for the future.

So do we!

We were hoping you'd say that.

In fact, we're here to ask for your help.

Us? Really?

What can WE do?
We're only kids.

We thought you might like to
EXPLORE the world with us...

brainstorm ideas...

...and share what you learn with others.

GREENHOUSE GASES

I'm in!

Where do we start?

Right here, in this book!

Each chapter tells a different story about what's going on...

...and how EVERYONE has a part to play.

Can we really help the whole planet?

Yes you can!

CONTENTS

Chapter 1 – page 7
CAN WE REALLY HELP THE POLAR BEARS?
Where we find out why the ice caps are melting, what that means for the rest of our planet and how we can stop it from warming up too much.

We make a GREAT plan.

Chapter 2 – page 53
CAN WE REALLY HELP THE BEES?
Where we meet the bees and other pollinators, learn all about food chains and find better ways to share our planet.

Look out for my awesome doodles.

Chapter 3 – page 97
CAN WE REALLY HELP THE TREES?
Where the forest animals explain what's happening to their homes, how important trees are for the whole planet, and what we can do to protect them.

You get to meet us in this chapter.

I'm carbon.

And we're oxygen.

Chapter 4 – page 143
CAN WE REALLY HELP THE DOLPHINS?
Where we dive into some amazing watery worlds and discover why a healthy planet needs a healthy ocean.

My video gets shared around the world.

GLOSSARY – page 188
Where you can look up some of the key words in this book.

Scan the QR code on the the back cover of this book for links to great websites about helping our planet.

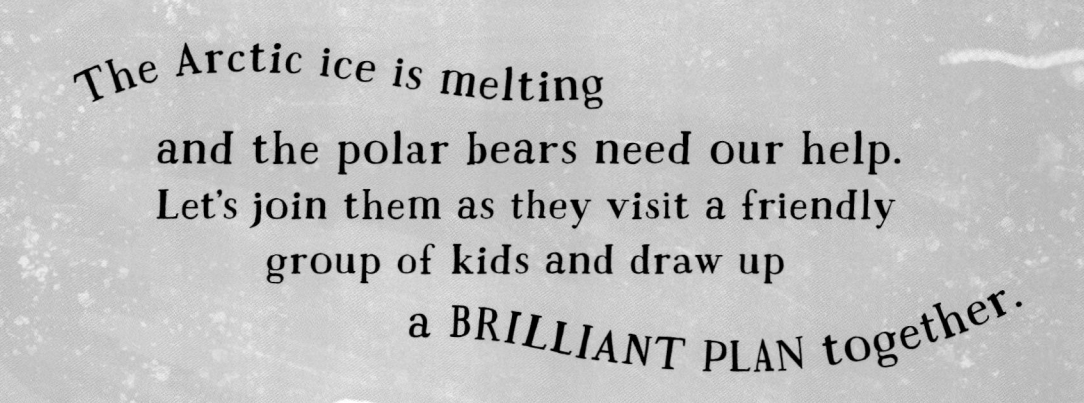

The Arctic ice is melting and the polar bears need our help. Let's join them as they visit a friendly group of kids and draw up a BRILLIANT PLAN together.

~ Chapter 1 ~
CAN WE REALLY HELP THE POLAR BEARS?

Yes you can!

Right, I've checked the map. Everyone ready?

Let's go!

ARCTIC

There's much less ice than last year.

From the Arctic

Dear Children,
WE NEED YOUR HELP!
We're heading South to explain why.
Please tell your friends.
See you soon.
Love from,

The Polar Bears

P.S. This is serious!

NORTH
SOUTH

The Children
Helpful Road
WARM LAND

Wow – real polar bears coming to visit US! We'd better get ready to welcome them!

8

Getting warmer
WARM LAND
Yuummm
It's berry snack time.
This farmer can give us a lift.
Beware of the smelly fumes!
It's getting warm now.
Let's cool off here.
YUCK! More smelly fumes...
...and dirty water!
I think we're nearly there...
Let's hope they got our letter.
KNOCK KNOCK
They're HERE!

IMPORTANT MEETING
Help the polar bears

Are they really here?

Yes, they're waiting in the living room.

And they want US to help THEM?

That's what their letter said...

I wonder why...

Thank you so much for having us.
We wouldn't normally bother you...

...but we've been having a tough time.

Why? What's wrong?

Cookie?

It's a long story...

We like stories!

You see, we're used to life in the freezing cold, hanging out on huge chunks of floating ice.

Brrrrr Sounds chilly!

It's not chilly for us in our thick fur coats.

The frozen Arctic is our home and the ice is our hunting ground.

When a tasty seal pokes its head above water...

...we POUNCE!

But now our home is MELTING.

And without the ice to hunt from, we're going to go VERY hungry.

Another cookie?

Yes please.

But WHY is the ice melting?

Well, it all started many years ago...

Ta dah!!

First, the STEAM ENGINE was invented.

chooo choooo

Then TRAINS.

Then POWER STATIONS for making electricity.

Then CARS, then PLANES.

All these inventions work by burning stuff called **FOSSIL FUELS.**

Fossils?

Like the ones you find on the beach?

Yes, a little like them.

I found a fossil with my Gran last summer.

Gran it's MASSIVE!

FUELS are things you burn to make heat or power.
And FOSSIL fuels are fuels made from
ancient plants and animals.

They've been squashed underground for millions of years

and have turned into

thick, black OIL

an invisible GAS

and dry, dusty COAL.

Humans dig up these fossil fuels from deep

deep

DEEP underground.

Then they burn them to release ENERGY so they can...

...heat homes.

...make electricity.

...power vehicles.

But when fossil fuels burn, they also release a gas called carbon dioxide, or CO_2 for short.

And THAT'S where the problem starts...

You see, CO_2 is a **GREENHOUSE** gas.

What's a GREENHOUSE gas?!

It's a gas that traps in heat.
It works like glass in a greenhouse.

Rays from the sun heat up the ground...

I know what a greenhouse is — my Gran has one!

...and the greenhouse traps in some of that heat.

It helps my plants to grow.

Greenhouses keep plants warm, and greenhouse gases keep our planet warm.

We need SOME greenhouse gases in the air around us.

BRRRRRR

Without them, the sun's heat would escape back into space.

And even the polar bears and penguins would freeze!

But adding MORE greenhouse gases is BAD NEWS.

They trap in MORE HEAT and make the planet WARM UP.

So THAT'S why your ice is melting! And why you can't hunt for seals.

Um, why don't you eat something else instead?

They don't have cookies in the Arctic.

This isn't just about feeding the polar bears. A warmer planet will affect ALL of us!

meow!

But if it gets warmer
we can play outside more!

We can go to the
beach and swim in the sea...

...even in winter!

I'm afraid warmer temperatures
AREN'T good news for everyone.

Already, they're causing
all kinds of problems...

In some places, **wild storms** are making too much wind and rain.

In other places, the sun is too HOT, the rain won't fall and forests are BURNING.

People and animals sometimes struggle to get the food they need.

Meanwhile, our seas are **rising**.

The seawater **expands** as it gets warmer and creeps up the land.

Melted ice runs off the mountains and fills up the sea **EVEN MORE**.

Homes and farms are getting **flooded**.

Baaaa!

HELP!

That's AWFUL!
What are we going to do?

Couldn't we just STOP making so much greenhouse gas?

Meow!

Great idea!

YES!

YES!

YES!

YES!

Sounds good... but HOW do we do that?!

We need a PLAN.

Let's make a list of the problems, then think up some solutions.

GREENHOUSE GASES

PROBLEMS

SOLUTIONS

Making electricity

Powering vehicles

Heating homes

I've forgotten – why is making electricity such a problem?

Because over half of the world's electricity comes from burning fossil fuels, making **LOTS of CO_2**.

Let's try to use LESS electricity then.

We can SWITCH THINGS OFF when we're not using them.

Hey, who unplugged the house?

Sorry Ma'am. We need to stop burning coal.

But there are also BETTER ways of making electricity in the first place.

27

You can make electricity from the **whizzing** of the wind...

the **shining** of the sun...

Wind turbine

Solar panel

...and the **whooshing** of water.

THEY don't create nasty fumes or greenhouse gases. So they're called **CLEAN ENERGY SOURCES.**

Let's use them then!

There's a house on my street with solar panels.

And wind turbines on the hill near me!

SOLUTIONS

CLEAN ENERGY

What about VEHICLES?
How do THEY make greenhouse gases?

By burning FUEL inside their engines, which gives off CO_2 and other nasty fumes.

Pooo-eey

My Uncle's got an ELECTRIC car. Is that any better?

YES! Because it doesn't burn fuel and make nasty gases.

CHARGING POINT

Charge up the car with electricity.

Electricity is stored in a battery.

Battery

Motor

The battery powers the motor and makes the wheels turn.

29

Electric cars don't puff out nasty fumes.

Let's make ALL vehicles electric!

And let's charge them up with electricity from CLEAN ENERGY SOURCES.

I'm going to invent a car that runs on WATER.

I love it!

We're going to use our own legs
and arms to get around.

Muscle power is a very
clean source of energy.

But it would take HOURS
to walk to my Gran's.

You could get a lift
with your cousins...

One car is better than two!

...or you could go by train.
Trains make MUCH less CO_2 per passenger than cars.

What about flying?

Not good, I'm afraid. One plane gives off the same amount of CO_2...

...as 200 fossil fuel cars making the same journey.

And some plane journeys can be VERY LONG.

So why don't we make ELECTRIC planes?

Inventors are trying to...

We need a HUGE battery to store enough electricity for take-off.

Um, where do the passengers go?!

Battery

It won't budge!

...but until we can make better batteries, electric planes won't take us very far.

Let's try to FLY LESS then, while we solve the plane problem.

My Auntie can do her business meetings online.

Italy USA Kenya

People can have adventures closer to home.

There's a campsite near me.

Great! Those solutions can go on the plan.

Powering vehicles

Share cars

Use muscle power

Trains NOT planes

Camping near home

33

What's the next problem?

HEATING HOMES. That makes lots of CO_2.

Powering vehicles
Trains NOT planes
Share cars
Use muscle power
Heating homes

Let's turn the heat down!

Brrr ...but I'll get cold!

Then put on a sweater.

Our house is ALWAYS cold.

You should put a sweater over the house!

I'm nearly there!

Actually, that's not as silly as it sounds.

Houses with extra padding keep in more heat.

The padding goes INSIDE the walls, so it doesn't get soggy.

It's called insulation.

Ooh toasty.

Insulation

And you can heat your homes with CLEAN ENERGY.

Why don't we just move to a warmer country?

If the world keeps getting warmer, we might not NEED heating!

Ah, but people in hot countries make greenhouse gases too, trying to COOL their buildings.

Hot
Cold

35

Air conditioning units use electricity to take heat out of the air.

Air conditioning unit

Why not close shutters instead, to block out the heat?

Or grow trees for shade?

And paint the walls white so the hot sun bounces off them.

Those are brilliant ways to keep cool without warming up the world.

Any more greenhouse gas makers?

What about FACTORIES? They look smoky and gassy.

Trees for shade

Wear a sweater

Yes, and the things they churn out can make even MORE greenhouse gas.

Use **CLEAN ENERGY** to make **EARTH-FRIENDLY THINGS**

Why do factories make so much stuff in the first place?

Because we keep BUYING it!

We should buy LESS then!

We're learning about the 3Rs in school...

REDUCE
I don't need ANOTHER top!

RE-USE
I can mend this one!

And if it's beyond repair...

RECYCLE

That's right.

If you make LESS new stuff in the first place you'll **really** help the planet.

More cookies anyone?

That reminds me... food is a greenhouse gas maker too.

Food?!

Yes, food can make lots of greenhouse gas.

Especially if it's flown in from faraway countries...

...or grown under heat lamps.

Oops, we made too much.

And if you throw food away, then that's bad too.

Why?

Because growing and preparing food makes CO_2 whether you eat it or not!

LANDFILL SITE

And burying food makes another greenhouse gas called METHANE.

FOOD PROCESSING

Gosh. I'd better finish what's on my plate.

REPAIR

buy less stuff

RE-USE

RECYCLE

39

Or you could cook up
your leftovers the next day.

My Gran puts her food
waste in a compost bin.

It turns into a rich soil
for my garden.

We love your Gran!

Mr. Polar Bear, is it true that
cows and sheep BURP OUT
greenhouse gas?

**Yes they do.
That's methane too.**

So it's not just OUR
fault that the planet
is getting warmer.

No way!

You should talk to the cows as well.

Excuse me, Mrs. Cow. Can you stop burping please?

Tee hee

The thing is, most cows are only here because humans want them for their meat or milk.

I love a chocolate milkshake.

I make a yummy beef stew.

So... should we stop eating meat?

Eating LESS beef and lamb would help. And you'd be helping the forests too.

The FORESTS? What have THEY got to do with meat?

41

They're being CUT DOWN to make space to grow and feed farm animals.

You see, you need **10 times** more land to farm BEEF...

Meat burger

...than you do to farm PLANTS.

Veggie burger

I like trees...

...but I think I like meat more.

It's not as if we need so many trees in the world.

YES WE DO!

We need LOTS of them. They're not just homes to amazing animals...

...they also **CLEAN THE AIR** for us!

They spend all day sucking up the CO_2 around them.

Then they store the C bit (carbon)...

...and let out the O_2 (which is oxygen, the gas we all need to breathe).

If you destroy a tree, the carbon turns into CO_2 again...

...but if you let it grow, it can suck up even more CO_2.

In that case, we must PROTECT our FORESTS.

And PLANT MORE TREES.

And do everything else on our plan!

Let's start right NOW!

We can check things off as we do them.

☐ Plant more trees.

☐ Eat less meat.

☐ Buy less stuff.

Remember to REDUCE   RE-USE    RECYCLE

☐ Eat food that's in season.
(Grown locally or sent by ship)

☐ Use electric vehicles...

COLD DAYS

☐ Wear a sweater.

HOT DAYS

Make some shade.

44

Use less energy.

ECO MODE

Share car rides.

Beep!

...powered by CLEAN ENERGY.

Use muscle power.

Switch things OFF.

Take the train, not the plane.

Chug chug

45

But we can only REALLY help the polar bears if EVERYONE joins in!

Let's tell our parents and teachers.

Emergency meeting for all parents and teachers

It's a problem we all need to solve.

We should write to big businesses too. They can make A LOT of CO_2.

Here's the company address.

GREENHOUSE PROBLEMS

Making electricity

Powering vehicles

Heating and cooling buildings

Factories

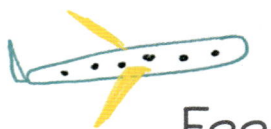

Food

Farming

FOSSIL FUELS

GASES
SOLUTIONS

- use CLEAN ENERGY
- switch things OFF
- use LESS energy

- walk or cycle
- go by train NOT plane
- car share
- use ELECTRIC vehicles (that run on CLEAN ENERGY)

- turn down the heat (and wear more clothes)
- add better insulation
- make more shade in hot countries

- make less stuff
- only use CLEAN ENERGY
- REDUCE, RE-USE, RECYCLE

- don't fly food around the world
- eat food that's in season
- don't waste food
- eat less meat

- protect our forests
- PLANT MORE TREES

LEAVE THEM IN THE GROUND

And talk to our politicians – they make the rules.

MEET YOUR POLITICIAN
9am - 11am

This is excellent. I'll tell the government.

Let's send copies of our plan to the leaders of EVERY country and big business IN THE WORLD!

There are nearly 200 countries.

YES! YES! YES!

47

We CAN
help the polar bears!

And you'll be helping the rest of the planet too.

Tweeeet!

YES!

THANK YOU!

Yippee!

Hooray!

Brilliant!

We'll deliver these on our way.

Great!

Take care.

Good luck.

President of the U.S.A.

Meow

Thanks so much for your help. Goodbye.

What next?

The problems the polar bears describe in this story are REAL and affect us ALL. The GOOD NEWS is that things are already changing...

In 2015, countries around the world agreed to work TOGETHER to stop the planet from warming up too much.

It's called the Paris Agreement, because it happened in Paris.

Sim   Yes   Oui   Ja   Yes   예   Yes   是   Ja

Over 30 countries have promised to STOP using coal for energy.

Over 20 countries have announced they will BAN fossil fuel vehicles in the future.

The sooner the better!

Solar panels and wind turbines are now a CHEAPER source of electricity than fossil fuel power stations.

New LED bulbs to light our homes use 10 times LESS energy than the old-fashioned ones.

There's still LOTS MORE TO DO and we'll all need to play our part to make a cleaner, greener future.

I'm going to be an INVENTOR and make a machine that sucks CO_2 out of the air.

I'm going to be a FOREST MANAGER and plant a billion native trees.

I'm going to be a WILDLIFE EXPERT and learn more about polar bears.

I'm going to set up a BUSINESS making water-powered cars.

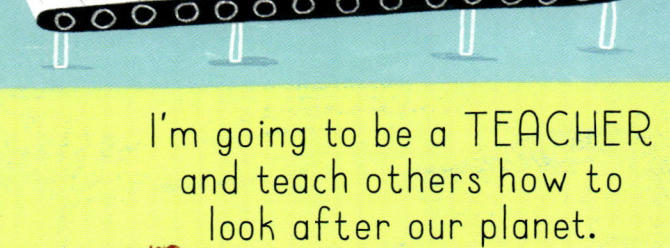

I'm going to be an ARCHITECT and design houses that run on clean energy.

I'm going to be a POLITICIAN and make laws to stop air pollution.

I'm going to be a TEACHER and teach others how to look after our planet.

The bees are in danger and they need US to protect their pollinating powers.

It's not just honey that's at stake, but the future of the whole planet!

~ Chapter 2 ~
CAN WE REALLY HELP THE BEES?

Yes you can!

Buzzzz

The bees have come to see us!

They're making a shape in the window.

It looks like a sad face.

And now they're making an arrow.

Ooh, let's follow them!

Where are they going?

No idea!

We're taking you to meet a queen.

A queen?!
The bees can talk!

She lives here, in a hole.

I thought bees lived in HIVES.

No, most of us make NESTS.

And over half of us live UNDERGROUND.

I lay my eggs inside a branch.

We look after our eggs and babies in here.

I lay my eggs down here, on balls of food.

They're safe underground.

Only HONEYBEES live in hives.

But aren't ALL bees honeybees?

We most certainly are not!

I'm a queen bumblebee.

Pleased to meet you, Your Majesty.

I'm a leafcutter bee.

I'm a mining bee.

I'm a carpenter bee.

And I really am a honeybee.

We saw your sad face and arrow.

Is something wrong?

I'm afraid so.
Our lives are in danger.

Oh no!

? ? ?

And we were hoping **YOU** could help us.

Like SUPERHEROES!

I suppose so...

Where's the danger?

Who are the bad guys?

Is it the wasps?

Should we **ZAP** them?

NO, wasps are fine.

wzzzzz!

wzzzzk!

Then what's the problem?

60

Ahem, er, hmm, actually HUMANS are the PROBLEM.

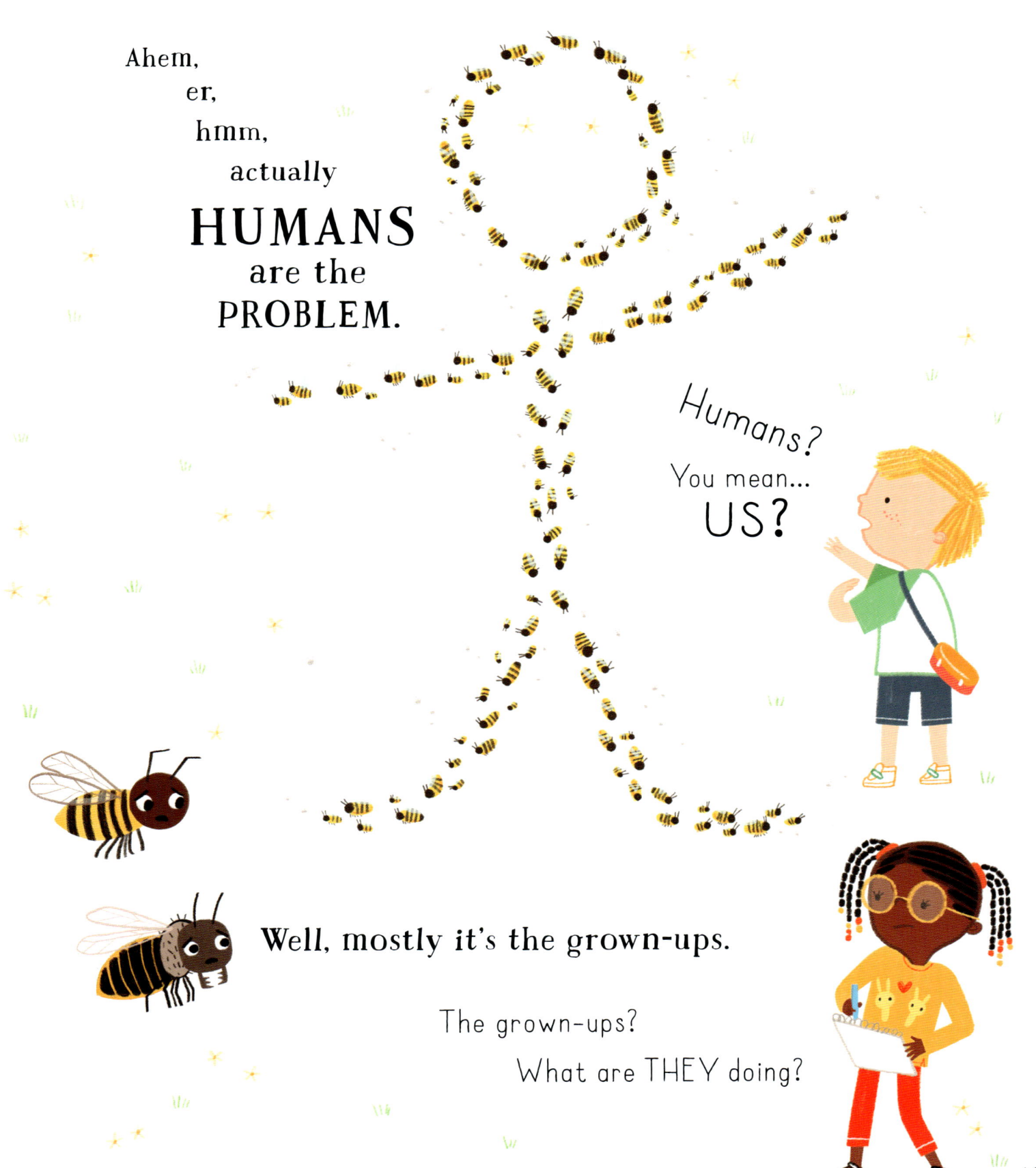

Humans? You mean... US?

Well, mostly it's the grown-ups.

The grown-ups?

What are THEY doing?

They're mowing down flowers.

Paving over natural spaces.

Spraying fields with harmful chemicals.

Chopping down forests.

BELCHING out fumes from their cars...

WE DELIVER ANYTHING

20 21 22

...and trucks.

COUGH COUGH

Soon we'll have nowhere to live and nothing left to eat.

And that will spell **TROUBLE** for LOTS of living things.

squawk!

T... R... O...
What comes after O?

HELP!
BANG

Gosh!

We'd LOVE to help you.

We can try our best.

But how does helping YOU help other living things?

It's not as if we really NEED honey.

And most of you don't even MAKE honey!

Hmmm... I guess we should tell you about our SUPERPOWER.

SUPERPOWER?

Can you turn *invisible*?

Are you faster than a rocket?

No, even better than that, we're
POLLINATORS.

Umm... what's a pollinator?

An animal that can spread POLLEN!

We buzz from flower to flower sucking sweet nectar, and spreading dusty POLLEN from inside the flowers.

Yummy nectar gives us energy.

Pollen sticks to our fuzz... ...and rubs off on other flowers.

Why is spreading pollen a superpower?!

Because plants CAN'T GROW without it.

They NEED pollen from another flower...

...so they can make their fruits and seeds.

And so that YOU have FOOD to eat, too.

I'm not a big fan of fruit. I prefer pizza.

Ah ha, but pizza wouldn't be pizza without us.

We pollinate the tomato flowers!

The PEPPERS too – that's us.

And the onions and yummy herbs...

Yep, us!

In fact **three-quarters** of the world's food crops need pollinators.

Even the COTTON your T-shirt is made of needed bees and other insects to grow.

Cotton flowers are pollinated by insects...

...then the flowers turn into balls of cotton.

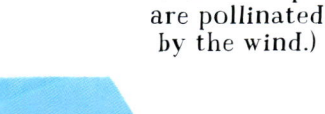

(Cereal crops are pollinated by the wind.)

Not to mention COFFEE.

It takes **25 trillion** flower visits by bees to make all the cups of coffee grown-ups drink in a year.

Pollinated coffee flowers turn into berries with coffee beans inside.

My Dad loves coffee!

Wow. Pollinating is a useful job!

67

But if pollinators like us no longer have places to live and flowers to feed from, then we'll all DIE!

And things will become much harder for the rest of you.

NO POLLINATORS CAFÉ

ICE CREAMS
- CHOC CHIP
- MANGO
- LEMON
- STRAWBERRY

JUICES
- APPLE
- RASPBERRY
- WATERMELON
- ORANGE

HOT DRINKS
- CAPPUCCINO
- LATTE
- HOT CHOCOLATE

SNIP SNIP

ZZZ

No more apple juice...

...or CHOCOLATE!

And no more coffee!

TWEET

But also no more fruits and seeds for birds and other animals to eat...

...and no more seeds to grow NEW plants.

You see, the lives of ALL living things are CONNECTED, so everyone will be affected.

For example...

We pollinate the PLANTS.

GRASSHOPPERS eat PLANTS.

MICE eat GRASSHOPPERS.

And HAWKS eat MICE!

You can draw arrows between who eats what. It's called a FOOD CHAIN.

squeak!

69

Plants are at the beginning of food chains. And food chains weave together to make a much bigger FOOD WEB, like this one.

CARROTS

FLOWERS

CLOVER

LEAVES

BUTTERFLY

CATERPILLAR

GRASSHOPPER

DRAGONFLY

MOUSE

Ribbit

FROG

FOX

RABBIT

GRASS

SHEEP

Baa!

APPLES

FLY

SPIDER

TROUT

CHICKEN

HUMAN

EGGS

HAWK

Squawk!

But without pollinators to help make NEW plants, many chains will BREAK DOWN...

...and other living things in the web will go hungry!

71

Then we need to
PROTECT THE POLLINATORS!

But Your Majesty, is there really NOWHERE left for you to live? I mean, the world is so BIG and you're so small...

Well, it's getting trickier for us as humans take over MORE and MORE of the planet with their buildings and roads and farms and mines and dumping places.

HUGE areas of forests and wild grasslands have already been destroyed.

In some places **90%** of the natural land has **GONE.**

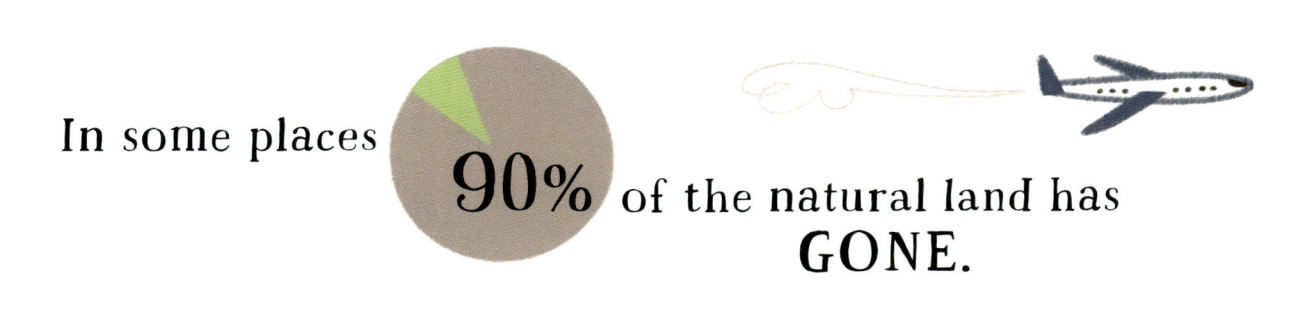

That's awful. What can we do?

Can't we just ~SHARE~ the land WITH you?

YES, PLEASE!

Why don't you share our FARMS?

Yes, farms grow LOTS of plants!

We'd love to, but many farms don't have homes for us anymore.

Trees, hedges and wildflowers have been cleared away to make BIGGER fields for BIGGER tractors.

And many farmers use CHEMICAL SPRAYS. The chemicals help the plants to grow FASTER, and they kill off plant-munching PESTS.

But they *kill* BEES too!

Gulp!

Then who's left to pollinate the flowers?

No one!

Farmers either have to order in hives of honeybees...

HONEYBEE DELIVERY

The journey really stresses us out!

...or try to pollinate the flowers by hand!

That's bonkers!

And it's not just pollinators who are useful on farms. Worms, beetles and other animals help too.

PLEASE DON'T SPRAY US! WE'RE HERE TO HELP :)

We make the soil HEALTHY for growing new plants.

And we GOBBLE UP pests!

The organic blueberry farm near us grows wild flowers as well as blueberry bushes. Could you live there?

Yes, that sounds good.

But then the farmer has less space to grow blueberries.

That's OK. I can save money by not having to buy sprays or order in bee hives!

Great, so farmers can help the bees by sharing their land with them.

Hooray! We LOVE bee-friendly farms.

But how can other people help?
Would you like to share our towns and cities with us?

Yes, please.

As long as there is plenty of nature around.

We could plant more flowers for you.

In our parks.

And in our gardens.

And in our windowboxes.

Sounds lovely – thank you.

We could add more rooftop gardens...

...with beehives on them too.

Grow plants out of walls.

Make green bridges for nature.

And plant flowers on top of bus stops.

Awesome. That would really help.

You can also leave areas to grow wild by themselves.

We love to make nests in overgrown places.

And you could build us some bee hotels.

BEE HOTEL

Hotels? For bees?!

We don't need beds and showers, just some hollow wooden tubes would do!

What about trees?
Are they any good for bees?

Yes. Some of us LIVE in trees.
And we ALL love tree flowers.

Each tree only blooms for a short while...

February to March

April to May

...but different trees bloom at different times through the year.

So we should plant MORE trees.

Ones that grow well in our area.

And choose a range of tree types, so there's always one in bloom...

June to July

...whatever the season.

September to October

Excellent!

Are we getting closer to helping the bees?

YES!

The more trees the better.

Trees planted along streets help link up flower patches, so we can buzz from one to the next.

You see, some bees need to visit TWO THOUSAND flowers in a day.

That's a LOT of flowers!

How about growing more wildflowers along the sides of roads?

Good idea.

There are sooooo many roads, you could easily grow TWO MILLION flowers.

Or even two BILLION!

BEE HIGHWAY
NO MOWING
NO SPRAYING

We could create bee highways all around the country.

That would be wonderful!

But PLEASE can you stop *whizzing* along the roads in vehicles that give off harmful fumes?

They make us unwell.
COUGH!

Me too! They can trigger my asthma and make it hard for me to breathe.

I need to take my preventer inhaler twice a day to stay well.

83

The air would be much CLEANER for all of us if more people walked or cycled.

We should make lots more cycle tracks and footpaths.

Let's plant trees and flowers along the edges.

And only let ELECTRIC vehicles use the roads. They don't puff out harmful fumes.

Fresh air and nature make me happy!

Me too.

And me!

BEE HIGHWAY
NO MOWING NO SPRAYING

TOOT TOOT!

For longer journeys we could travel by bus or train.

A bus can carry more people than 10 cars.

And a train can carry more people than 100 cars!

Has anyone been writing this down. There's so much to remember!

Yes, I've been doodling it all. Here's what I've got...

85

Bees have an awesome SUPERPOWER...

We're POLLINATORS!

Bees SPREAD POLLEN.

Then flowers can turn into FRUITS with SEEDS.

Without pollinators we'd have **none** of these.

3/4 of all crops couldn't grow.

NO bees, no seeds, no new plants

I'm hungry.

I'll be hungry soon.

So will I!

Food chains would **break down**.

kzzzz

There's no food left!

There's nowhere to live!

grrrrrr

This is why bees are in TROUBLE.

tzzz

pssssz

INSECT KILLER

HELP!

BEE-FRIENDLY FARM

SHARE THE LAND

"I'll pollinate your flowers."

"I'll take care of the soil."

"I'll eat any pests."

"Thank you."

AND HERE ARE LOTS OF SOLUTIONS.

PLANT MORE FLOWERS

SEEDS

Trees for every season

GIVE BEES A HOME

Go wild. Don't mow – let it grow.

BEE HOTEL

← Leafcutter bee nest

← Bumblebee nest

↑ Honeybee hive

MAKE BEE HIGHWAYS

With bee-friendly vehicles

Wow, I think you've covered EVERYTHING!

We wish ALL humans knew what you know.

We should show EVERYONE the doodles.
Then they can learn about bees too!

My Auntie works at a printers.

She could make lots of copies.

GREEN PRINTING

HELP THE BEES!

HELP THE BEES!

We could hand them out after school.

And hopefully our friends will show their families too.

Let's send the doodles to a book publisher.

Positive Publisher
Green Street
Ecoville

Maybe they'll decide to print them!

More people need to know this!

The pictures are great.

Let's publish it!

POSITIVE PUBLISHER

It could become a BESTSELLER...

...in LOTS of countries!

HELP THE BEES!

救救蜜蜂!

HELFT DEN BIENEN!

POMÓŻMY PSZCZOŁOM!

AIDONS LES ABEILLES !

Βοηθήστε τις Μέλισσες!

벌을 도와주세요!

Yippee!

We're going to be FAMOUS!

91

We really CAN help the bees.

YAY!

And other pollinators too.

And all kinds of living things around the world...

...including humans!

Thank you so much.

Thank YOU for all your amazing pollinating.

I'll think of you when I eat my pizza tonight.

Goodbye!

What next?

The problems the bees describe in this story are REAL and affect us ALL.
BUT the GOOD NEWS is that things are already changing...

More and more cities are sowing seeds to become POLLINATOR FRIENDLY.

NATIONAL POLLINATOR PLAN

Many governments now have POLLINATOR PLANS, to increase the number of bees and other pollinators in their countries.

Lots of farmers are now paid to keep or restore wildflower meadows on their land.

Welcome to our
BEE SAFE COUNTRY.
NO SPRAY HERE

Many countries around the world have already BANNED the use of bee-killing sprays.

Bee charities are working hard to spread the word and all kinds of people are getting involved.

There's still LOTS MORE TO DO and we can all play a part in supporting pollinators and other wildlife.

I'm going to be a TEACHER and help others to learn about bees.

I'm going to be a FARMER and make my farm a haven for wildlife.

Nature-friendly Flowerfilled Farm

I'm going to be a SCIENTIST and study pollinators, so I can think up more ways to help them.

I'm going to be a POLITICIAN and make laws to ban harmful chemicals.

I'm going to be a CRAFTSPERSON and build homes for bees and other minibeasts.

I'm going to be a LANDSCAPE ARCHITECT, designing city parks for pollinators.

Saving the world's forests is never going to be easy...

...but with a jaguar, an orangutan, two bear cubs and a squirrel to show the way, ANYTHING is possible!

~ Chapter 3 ~

CAN WE REALLY HELP THE TREES?

Yes you can!

RUSTLE

RUSTLE

Does anyone else feel like we're not alone?

I can see a pair of eyes.

And a spotted tail.

And an orange beard.

Hey, who's out there?

Woah.
Is that a leopard?

I'm a jaguar, actually.

Wow, you can talk!

And are you a... gorilla?

No, I'm an orangutan.

Um, nice to meet you!

We're just having some snacks.
Would you like to join us?

Yes, please.
I've had a long journey and I'm starving.

Me too!

KNOCK KNOCK

MORE visitors?

Hello! Oooh, snacks.

Wait for me!

Hello. Welcome to our treehouse.

Thank you. We're sorry to intrude, but we're here with an important message.

Who from?

The trees.

The TREES?
You mean the tall branchy things?

Yes, of course.

But trees don't send messages...

FORESTS OF THE WORLD

BOREAL FORESTS
RAINFORESTS
COOLER WOODLANDS
WARMER WOODLANDS

And WE don't normally travel thousands of miles to have snacks in a treehouse, but THIS IS SERIOUS!

The trees are in danger. They need YOU to protect them.

US?

Protect the TREES?

But they're so much bigger and stronger than us.

Not when they're CHOPPED DOWN they're not.

Nor when they're BURNED to the ground.

But trees are just PLANTS, aren't they?

Well yes...

So it's OK to chop or burn them down, isn't it?

NO IT'S NOT!

OK, so it wasn't exactly the trees who sent us.
We came because WE are in danger too.

HELP

You see, the trees are our HOME.
And millions of other living
things depend on trees too.

Do jaguars REALLY
live in trees?

CRRICKLE   CRRACKLE

Yes, in and
around them. We're excellent climbers.

Jaguars live in the Amazon rainforest, in South America.

A rainforest is a steamy jungle crawling with life. One in ten of all the world's plant and animal species live here.

There are thousands of different trees, from GIANT kapoks...

...to little cacao trees – where your chocolate comes from.

Chatty macaws and bright-beaked toucans fly through the leaves.

KAKORR

Spider monkeys hang by their tails.

And three-toed sloths hug onto branches. (They only climb down once a week, for a toilet trip!)

The Amazon rainforest is HUGE... but it's getting smaller every year.

Vast areas are being cut down or burned...

GRRRZZ

...mostly to make fields for beef cattle, or to grow soy beans.

CRRICKLE

And all the wonderful animals, plants and people of the rainforest are left with nowhere to live.

SQUELP

squark

CRRACKLE

SOY BEANS

That's AWFUL. I'm so sorry.

Mr. Orangutan, are you from the Amazon too?

No, my rainforest is on an island called Borneo, in Southeast Asia.

Borneo is home to the rhinoceros hornbill...

...and the Malaysian flying fox.

I'm not really a fox. I'm a big bat.

Pygmy elephants weave among the trees...

...and Sunda pangolins make dens in tree hollows.

The world's largest flower, rafflesia, grows here.

It's very smelly!

And many life-saving medicines come from rainforest plants.

Wow.

Where the forest meets the sea, the mangrove trees grow.

Proboscis monkeys leap through their branches...

...while young fish, crabs and mudskippers shelter in their loopy roots.

But our forests are shrinking too.

People cut down the mangroves to farm juicy shrimps to eat.

They bulldoze roadways through our rainforest.

And they clear vast areas to plant row after row of palm oil trees.

What's PALM OIL?

It's a kind of vegetable oil used in over half of all supermarket products.

Sounds useful!

SWEET TREATS   PACKAGED FOOD   CLEANING STUFF   BEAUTY PRODUCTS

So why don't you make your home in the palm trees instead?

We've tried, but we got hungry and sick.

Palm oil plantations don't have the range of fruit, leaves, bark and insects we need to eat.

It's like asking you guys to eat nothing but cherries!

I've got a tummy ache.

Hmm, I see what you mean.

This is sounding BAD.

Where do you two bears live?

In the snowy boreal forest.

Never heard of it!

FORESTS OF THE WORLD

KEY — BOREAL FORESTS, RAINFORESTS

It's in blue on your map.

It's the COLDEST forest on Earth.
Well actually it's many forests, stretching across Canada, Northern Europe and Russia.

Moose,

snowshoe hares,

wolves

and pine martens live here...

...as well as owls, ravens and crossbill birds.

But the boreal trees are being cut down too.

Humans use their wood for buildings and furniture – and for making a pulp that can be turned into paper.

SAW SAW

CHIP CHIP

SQUISH, SQUELCH, MIX TO GOO

SQUEEZE & ROLL

BRAND NEW PAPER

And it's not just the faraway forests that are in trouble. Trees near you are being chopped down too.

In fact, the world has lost **HALF ITS TREES** since human beings came along.

BEFORE HUMANS

NOW

Gulp.

This is terrible!

But WE need somewhere to live too. And space to grow our food...

Yes, but you also NEED TREES.

Not just for building treehouses in, but for helping the whole planet.

Trees help the planet?

YES! They give shelter from heavy rain...

...and SHADE from the sun.

Their roots hold the soil in place...

...and soak up water, which stops places from flooding.

No LANDSLIDES!

No FLOODS!

Lots of lovely soil for new plants to grow!

Trees also CLEAN THE AIR.
They absorb harmful gases and tiny particles – like the ones your cars and chimneys puff out.

NO.1 WORLD'S BEST AIR CLEANER

In particular, they soak up the BIG TROUBLEMAKER, carbon dioxide.

Carbon who?

Carbon dioxide, or CO_2 for short.

I'm C for carbon.

And we're O for oxygen.

Together we make CO_2.

CO_2 is a gas given off when humans burn fuels, such as coal and oil...

...in power stations, factories, vehicles and homes.

The trouble is, CO_2 traps the sun's heat, making the whole planet **warmer** and harder to live on.

YIKES!

So... how do trees help?

Our weather is going **WILD!**

They take in CO_2 from the air through their leaves...

...and store the C bit (carbon) in their branches, trunks and roots.

Then they give off the O_2 part...

...which is oxygen, the gas we all need to breathe.

Cool!

119

But if you cut down trees

or burn them...

NO.1 WORLD'S BEST AIR CLEANER

...the carbon is released and becomes CO_2 again. And then the world gets EVEN HOTTER.

Why don't we PLANT MORE TREES to replace the ones we cut down?

Then the new trees could soak up the carbon again!

That would be helpful.

Can't we just **STOP DESTROYING** forests and woodlands in the first place?

YES!

YES!

YESSS!

YES!

Great idea. But where do we even begin?

Let's start by looking at WHY people are chopping down trees.

We need wood from trees for buildings, furniture and paper.

And for all those PACKAGES your deliveries come in.

There must be ways for us to use LESS WOOD.

Why don't we...

...REPAIR old furniture rather than throwing it away.

...RECYCLE the paper and cardboard we use.

...write on both sides of the paper, so we only use half as much!

These are good ideas.

You can also buy RECYCLED paper.

Look out for this symbol.

My dad buys recycled toilet paper.

Ugh that's gross!

It's not the toilet paper that's recycled! It's made from other used paper.

Whew!

RECYCLE → SORT → SQUISH, SQUELCH MIX TO GOO → SQUEEZE & ROLL → RECYCLED TOILET PAPER / RECYCLED PAPER

Can we KEEP ON making new paper out of old paper?

No, it loses its quality. You can only recycle it roughly four times.

Hmm. So we'll still need wood from trees to make NEW paper.

Yes, but we could get the wood by growing NEW trees. Then we don't need to touch the beautiful old forests!

Tweet

PROTECTED ANCIENT WOODLAND

What about making things from bamboo instead? Is that any good?

YES!

Bamboo is great. It grows REALLY FAST, and when you cut it down, it grows again.

Is bamboo a tree?

It's so tall!

No, it's a GRASS!

But people shouldn't clear away TREES to plant the bamboo!

Where can we grow it instead?

Almost anywhere. Its strong roots are good for the soil. But choose NATIVE bamboo plants – ones that already come from the area.

And don't just grow it on its own. We need a HEALTHY MIX of plants to keep the animals HAPPY!

WELL SAID!

HEALTHY PLANTS
HAPPY ANIMALS

In Mexico, big food companies are clearing lush forests to plant only avocado trees.

AVOCADOS ONLY FARM

Avocados are making us lots of money. We want you to plant MORE!

But they're soaking up all our water!

My dad says avocados are a SUPERFOOD.

Hmm. They're not so super for the forest plants and animals that are left with nowhere to live.

HELP!

I've kept the avocado seed. Can I grow my OWN avocado tree?

You could try!

Or you could buy avocados that come from forest-friendly farms.

Mr. Orangutan, what can we do about the palm oil farms that are ruining YOUR forest?

Don't we NEED the palm oil for our supermarket food?

Hmmm. Well it's useful, cheap and hard to avoid.

These snacks are all likely to contain palm oil.

Oh dear.

My cookie recipe doesn't have palm oil in it. We could make our own instead of buying them!

Yay!

People can also grow palm oil and other things in a SUSTAINABLE way.

What does SUSTAINABLE mean?

It means growing crops without damaging forests or hurting nature along the way.

SUSTAINABLE FARMING GUIDE

- No burning ☐
- Protect the soil ☐
- Keep a variety of plants ☐
- Be friendly to wildlife ☐
- Be fair to local people ☐

But how do we KNOW if the palm oil is sustainable?

Some products now tell you in the list of ingredients.

Oh that's useful. We should make ALL food companies tell us where their ingredients are from...

...and if they're sustainable or not!

How can we help your Amazon, Miss Jaguar?

I suppose the CATTLE need to live somewhere.

Moooo!

FORESTS OF THE WORLD

BOREAL FORESTS
RAINFORESTS
COOLER WOODLANDS
WARMER WOODLANDS

Well, the fact is there wouldn't BE so many cattle if humans ate less BEEF!

What should we eat instead? Chicken?

Maybe. But our rainforest is also being chopped down to grow soy beans to feed chickens!

There's lots of protein in a soy bean.

Yikes.
So what can we eat instead?
Dad says WE need protein, too.

Strangely enough, it would be better if YOU ate the soy beans, rather than feeding them to animals then eating the animals.

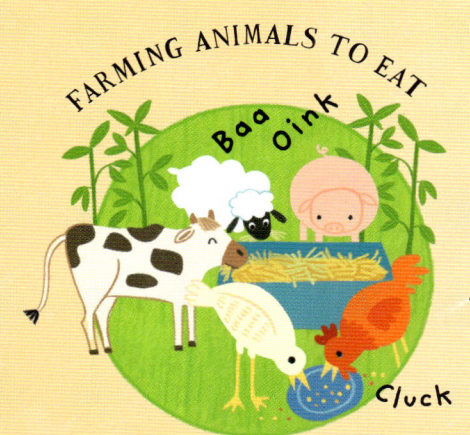

FARMING ANIMALS TO EAT

Baa   Oink

Cluck

How come?!

Because farming plant protein takes up MUCH LESS SPACE than farming the same amount of protein from animals!

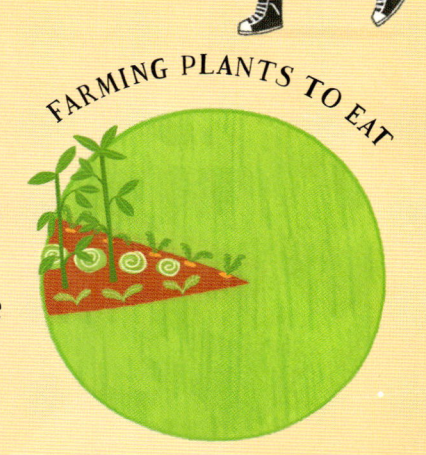

FARMING PLANTS TO EAT

So... if we eat less meat, there will be more land to grow TREES!

My plant burgers are delicious!

Whoop!

Yay!   Hooray!

Yes!

129

Hey, if we leave the forests alone, can the damaged areas grow back again?

Yes!

Let nature be and it can heal itself and spread further. It's called REWILDING.

Seeds from trees plant themselves and new trees grow.

Other plants start growing too, and animals arrive to make new homes.

Don't clear away rotting trunks and branches. They make great homes for all kinds of living things.

Some trees need a little help from us to sow their seeds.

I swallow yummy fruits and spit out the large seeds.

I eat fruit too... and plant their seeds in my droppings!

I bury acorns to eat in the winter. But some stay buried... and grow into big oak trees.

Maybe WE could sow seeds too.

Let's REWILD our gardens...

and our parks...

...and our parking spaces!

Yes, please!

But to really make a difference we need EVERYONE
to understand what's so great about trees...
and what we can ALL do to help.

We could make posters to put up around our school and town.

Don't destroy trees

Treeeees
HELP US breeeathe

Trees keep our planet COOLER

MORE trees = LESS flooding

RECYCLE paper
and use RECYCLED paper

CHECK THE LABELS

- ☐ No palm oil
- ☐ Made of recycled paper
- ☐ Forest-friendly
- ☐ Sustainable
- ☐ Plant-based
- ☐ Can be recycled

LET PLANTS GROW

They help the soil

"I've got a home again."
"Us too!"

Plant MORE trees

Choose a range of native trees

RE-USE

REPAIR old furniture

Eat less meat

Eat more beans and veggies = more room for trees

REWILD

Before

After

PROTECT the TREES

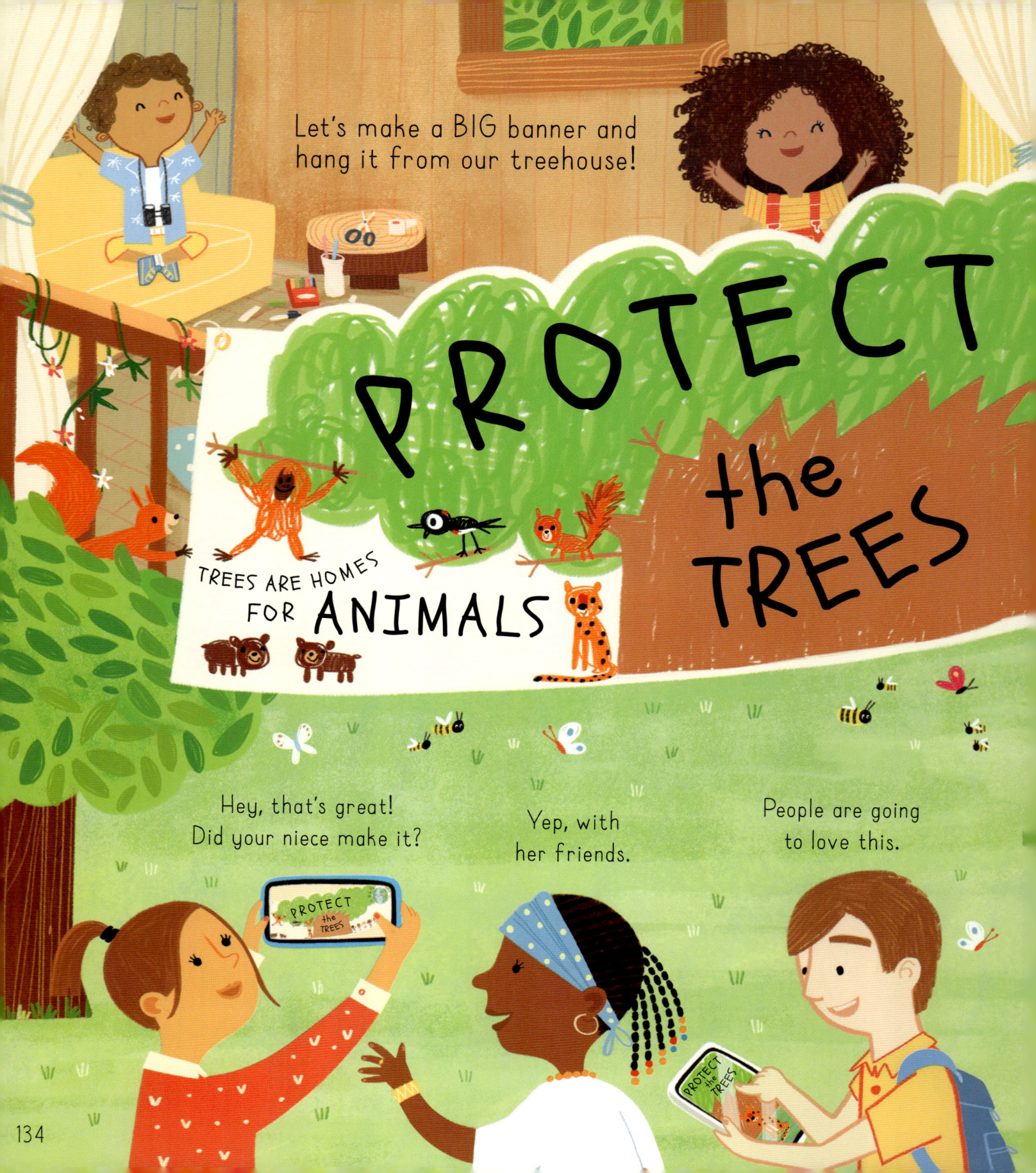

Let's make a BIG banner and hang it from our treehouse!

TREES ARE HOMES FOR ANIMALS

Hey, that's great! Did your niece make it?

Yep, with her friends.

People are going to love this.

THEY LOOK AFTER
THE PLANET
AND
THEY LOOK AFTER US

The local news might find out about it and come to interview us!

Can you tell us why you made your banner?

We'd love to!

Other children might hear about us and decide to do their own banners.

That's so cool. WE should make one!

We can help the trees too!

Together, we'll spread the word **AROUND THE WORLD!**

Wow!

Kids can really make a difference!

¡Guau!

¡Genial!

Then LOTS of people will join our campaign...

SAVE OUR FORESTS

...and governments and big businesses will have to listen and TAKE ACTION!

VOTE FOR THE TREE PARTY

We'll only get elected if we look after nature.

Our election strategy

MAKE ALL FOOD FOREST-FRIENDLY

BRANDING MEETING

People will only buy our products if they're sustainable.

BEST CEREAL EVER

PROTECT the TREES

TREES ARE HOMES FOR ANIMALS

THEY LOOK AFTER THE PLANET AND THEY LOOK AFTER US

SAVE THE PLANET!

We really CAN help the trees.

And our animal friends.

And you'll be helping the rest of the world too.

Including humans!

Number ONE world's best air cleaner

YAY!

Thank you so much.
Goodbye!

Goodbye and good luck!

Safe journey!

Come back and visit any time.

What next?

The problems the animals describe in this story are REAL and affect us ALL. But the GOOD NEWS is that things are already changing...

CLIMATE SUMMIT — **WE CAN DO THIS, IF WE ACT NOW**

Yay! Hooray! Whoop!

Over 100 countries have promised to end the destruction of forests and help them to grow back instead.

Some countries have also promised lots of money to help protect and restore our major forests.

We'd like to give millions to your rewilding project.

Forests the size of France have regrown over the last 20 years, thanks to restoration projects and more responsible farming.

Large land owners are choosing to plant millions of trees and create new woodlands.

TREES FOR LIFE! THIS IS OUR COMMUNITY ORCHARD CREATED WITH THE HELP OF LOCAL VOLUNTEERS

Wildlife charities are working hard to protect our trees, from the ones in cities to huge forests.

FOREST FOR THE FUTURE

There's still LOTS MORE TO DO and we can all play a part in protecting our trees, woodlands and forests.

I'm going to be an ECOLOGIST and discover which plants and animals need the most protection.

HIMALAYAN FIR TREE

I'm going to be a PARK RANGER and help people to respect and treasure our trees.

I'm going to be a BOTANIST and go on expeditions to discover new trees.

I'm going to set up a FOREST-FRIENDLY BUSINESS, making tree-free paper!

BANANA PEEL PRODUCTS

BANANA PAPER

WE MUST PROTECT TREES

I'm going to be a POLITICIAN and make laws to protect our trees and woodlands.

141

A message in a bottle turns a trip to the seaside into a worldwide campaign to SAVE the OCEAN.

It's time to meet the dolphins... and discover what's really going on under the sea.

~ Chapter 4 ~
CAN WE REALLY HELP THE DOLPHINS?

Yes you can!

Have you found anything interesting?

Some pretty shells and a fossil.

Ooh, here's something exciting.
No, wait – it's just a plastic bottle.
But there's a roll of paper inside...

It could be an important message.

Ah-hargh!

Maybe it's a cry for help from a shipwrecked pirate!

Or an invitation to a mermaid's party.

Don't be silly.

Gulp – actually...
it's from...
a dolphin.

A dolphin?
Who's the one being
silly now!

What does it say?

Dear Kids on Land,

Our home is in danger and we think YOU can help. We'll come to your pier to tell you more.

See you on the longest day of the year.

Yours gratefully,
Dolphin and Friends

The longest day... that's TODAY!

Quick! Let's go to the pier.

"You're here!"

"Wow, talking dolphins!"

"We were worried you wouldn't come."

"We got your letter. Are you really in danger?"

"I'm afraid so."

"You're a turtle!"

"I know."

We were hoping you could protect us.

A penguin! I LOVE penguins!

What do you need protecting FROM?

Well, lots of things really. Fishing nets, dirty water, harmful litter...

Like this plastic bottle?

Yes, plastic is one of the worst things!

What's so bad about plastic?

IT NEVER ROTS AWAY.

Plastic litter builds up in the sea and drifts even to the most faraway shores.

Sea creatures get tangled in it, or swallow it by mistake.

Yikes! Let me help.

Over time, plastic breaks into smaller pieces, but it DOESN'T disappear.

I can see lots of tiny pieces in the seawater.

They're called microplastics.

But it's not just plastic that's bothering us. Humans make all kinds of things that POLLUTE the sea.

What does POLLUTE mean?

It means SPLURGING OUT dirty, harmful stuff, from oil and chemicals to toilet waste.

Toilet waste? That's GROSS!

Imagine what it's like to swim in.

No thank you!

But the sea is our HOME and when it's not being spoiled by humans, it's an AMAZING place to live.

There are floating icy islands...

...and deep blue sea as far as the eye can see.

Animals of all shapes and sizes live here...

from tiny pink krill, to the biggest animals that ever lived...

...blue whales.

Wooooo ooo ooo

Seabirds dive to catch their dinner.

Small animals shelter in coral reef cities.

And shimmering schools of fish twist and turn and travel to new places.

It's so beautiful.

The deeper you go, the darker it gets and the stranger the creatures.

How BIG is the sea?

Arctic Ocean
Atlantic Ocean
Pacific Ocean
Indian Ocean
Southern Ocean

It's **ENORMOUS!**

The world's seas and oceans all flow into each other, making one gigantic ocean.

It covers over **70%** of the Earth's surface.

But our ocean is becoming really hard to live in. That's why we need your help.

What can WE do?

We're not the ones POLLUTING your ocean.

We all live hundreds of miles from the sea. We're only visiting for the summer.

Ahh, but you're much more connected to the sea than you realize.

We are?

Yes!

If litter on your street blows away or washes down a drain, where do you think it ends up?

Underground?

Maybe at first, but then it flows into a river.

Quack

And where do rivers end up?

Ooo, the sea!

Exactly!

And where do you think the
fish you eat comes from?

The sea!

Yes!

Is eating fish a problem?
I mean, there must be
ZILLIONS of fish in the sea.

It wouldn't be a problem,
if humans caught fish
RESPONSIBLY.

But selling fish
and other seafood is
BIG BUSINESS.
Fishing companies are
using bigger ships
and bigger nets
and they're sifting more and
more wildlife from the sea.

If this carries on, we'll ALL be in BIG trouble.

The ocean might RUN OUT of fish...

...and be filled with PLASTIC instead!

That would be TERRIBLE.

Did you know, you're also connected to the sea by the air you breathe.

No way!

Yes way!

You need OXYGEN from the air to LIVE...

...and over half the world's oxygen comes from the sea.

It bubbles up from seaweed forests and seagrass meadows.

Oxygen also bubbles out of tiny living things called PLANKTON.

Here are some plankton made 50 times bigger.

There are vast crowds of plankton drifting in the ocean's tides and currents.

How do plankton and other things make oxygen?

Funnily enough, oxygen is what they GET RID OF when they make their own food.

They take in WATER and a gas called CARBON DIOXIDE from the ocean...

CO_2

Yum yum!

...and use SUNLIGHT to turn them into a sugary food.

OXYGEN is what's left over.

Oxygen is O_2 for short, and carbon dioxide is CO_2.

O_2

It bubbles out for the rest of the planet to use.

Ooh, thanks plankton!

How does the carbon whatsit get INTO the ocean?

Carbon dioxide? It dissolves into the seawater from the air.

CO_2 CO_2 CO_2 CO_2

In fact, the seaweeds, seagrasses and plankton do a great job of taking in LOTS of the carbon dioxide made by humans.

CO_2 CO_2 CO_2
Whooooo

Oooh is that the gas we breathe out?

We can't help that!

Breathing out CO_2 is fine.
The problem comes when lots of
EXTRA CO_2 is added to the air.
It's made by burning coal, oil and gas...

to power your vehicles...

your factories...

...and your homes.

But MORE CO_2 should make the plankton happy!

Not really.
There's a limit on how much CO_2 the plankton can absorb. Too much CO_2 makes the water more ACIDIC.

Acidic?

Yes. Acids are sour liquids, like lemon juice. And acidic water isn't nice to live in.

It ruins our shells.

Ours too.

We need our shells to protect us.

It weakens our coral reefs.

Yuck, too much acid.

It makes it harder for our babies to grow.

Ugh!

And it can also harm those tiny oxygen-makers, plankton!

Oh no!

Then there's the even bigger problem of CLIMATE CHANGE.

I've heard grown-ups talking about that.

HELP!

I think it's why my uncle's house flooded last year.

And why there were forest fires in Australia.

FIRE! EVACUATE!

But WHY is climate change happening?

The main reason for climate change is TOO MUCH CO_2 in the air.

It traps the sun's heat, making our planet and its oceans WARM UP too much.

Oooh warmer water to swim in – that sounds nice.

It's not so nice for the animals and plants.

Even a small temperature change can mean we struggle to survive.

Polar animals need freezing cold weather or the ice melts and they can't hunt for food.

That's right!

And if snow and ice on the land melt too, the meltwater runs into the sea and makes the sea level rise.

Water is already lapping up higher around islands and seaside towns.

Meanwhile, the air above is getting **WILDER**.

Moist, hot air rises quickly above the warm ocean and swirls around making huge, powerful storms.

We can't enjoy the beach if it's stormy or flooded.

Or polluted with yucky things.

And we don't want the sea creatures to die!

We must
PROTECT OUR SEAS AND OCEANS.

Let's STOP MAKING TOO
MUCH CARBON DIOXIDE.

And all the other kinds
of POLLUTION!

YES!
YES!
YES!

And let's STOP CATCHING
TOO MANY FISH.

YES!
YES!
YES!

YES!

YES!

YES!

Woof!

YES!

YES!

Um, HOW are we going to manage all these things?!

Do we have to stop eating fish?

No, fish is good for you.

But gigantic nets are BAD because they catch **WHOLE SCHOOLS** of fish and put entire species in danger.

And heavy nets called bottom trawlers are bad too, because they scrape and ruin the ocean floor.

We must have caught a million today.

Oh no, they trap dolphins and turtles, too!

Why don't fishing companies use rods or smaller nets, so they don't take so many fish at once?

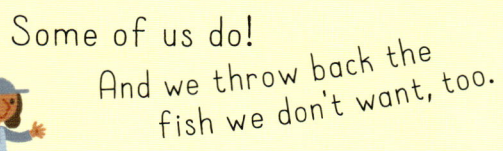

Some of us do! And we throw back the fish we don't want, too.

YAY!

This makes fishing more SUSTAINABLE.

What does sustainable mean?

Not taking too many of the same kind of fish...

...so there will always be more in the future.

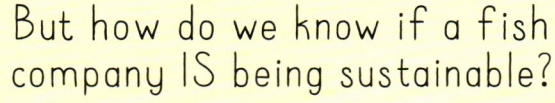

But how do we know if a fish company IS being sustainable?

Often there's a label on their packaging telling you.

CERTIFIED SUSTAINABLE SEAFOOD

Inspectors check up on the companies and only award labels to the sustainable ones.

Great. This packet is OK to buy.

169

What about all the plastic filling up the sea?

Why don't people take their litter home with them?

Beats me!

And why are so many things made of plastic in the first place?

Because it's waterproof and tough, it can be made into all shapes and sizes, and it can last for ages.

But it's bonkers to make stuff we throw away out of something that lasts for AGES!

We know!

50 years and it's still here!

My aunt avoids plastic packaging by buying things in glass jars.

We always take our own bags to the supermarket.

Our TV came in packaging made from mushrooms!

Excellent!

Thinking differently about what you buy and how you buy it can make a BIG difference.

Perhaps we could organize a BEACH CLEAN to clear up litter before it's washed into the ocean.

Yes please!

Thanks for joining us!

BEACH CLEAN HERE TODAY
Everyone welcome

What about other pollution?

How do we stop yucky stuff like sewage from reaching the sea?

This tanker has run aground and the oil is spilling out.

Let's make a BIG FUSS about it. Tell the people in charge that it's RUINING our ocean, making people UNWELL and KILLING our sea creatures.

Chemicals from this farm are seeping straight into the river.

This harmful dye is leaking from a clothes factory.

Would they listen to us?

It's worth a try!

Lots of people would be shocked and angry if they knew what's REALLY going on.

Woof!

I know... I'll make a VIDEO about it!

Thank you.
We really appreciate your help.

The trickiest problem is how to stop climate change.

It seems TOO BIG and complicated for us to solve.

But it's quite simple really.

Burn LESS
✗ coal
✗ oil
✗ gas

We just need to stop making extra CO_2. Then it can't trap in heat and warm up our planet!

Well when you put it like that...

174

There are BETTER ways to power our vehicles and homes.

Like the shining of the SUN!

The whizzing of the WIND!

The whooshing of WATER!

And our own muscle power!

Brilliant!
There's lots of wind power out at sea.

And you can use the power of the waves and the tides as well.

My dad is designing a container ship with sails. It runs on wind power instead of burning oil.
HOORAY!

Also, making less carbon dioxide means less acidy water.

And happier shellfish.

That's better!

Some divers recently found a happy, healthy coral reef that's deeper than the others.

We're happy because it's cooler down here.

Ooh, that's interesting.

We're all going to have to adapt a bit to cope with changes in the climate.

But if humans can stop the world from warming up TOO much...

...then climate change won't be so bad.

People are planting lots of trees on land to help SLOW DOWN climate change.

Can we do something like that in the water?

TREE PLANTING

YES!

You can plant things like seagrass meadows and mangrove swamps.

They trap carbon in their roots and make more oxygen.

And they protect coastlines from flooding too.

Let's mention this in the video.

I'm writing a TO DO list for the people in charge.

TO DO
* Clean up sewage
* Make laws on fishing
* Ban throwaway plastic
* Plant more seagrass

Great!

Sometimes the best thing to do is NOTHING – and let nature take back control.

BRUMMM BRUMMM

A beautiful sandy cove near me was so popular with tourists and their speedboats that the wildlife almost disappeared.

Then the locals closed it to visitors to let nature recover...

NO MOORING

...and within months dozens of blacktip reef sharks came back to swim in the bay!

Humans are allowed back now, but with strict rules on how many and where they can go.

I guess speedboats aren't great for nature.

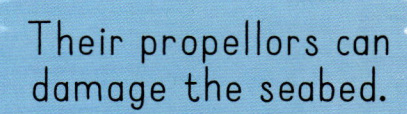

BRUMMM GRRRZzzz

Their propellors can damage the seabed.

And they're VERY NOISY.

I've got loads of great footage for a video now!

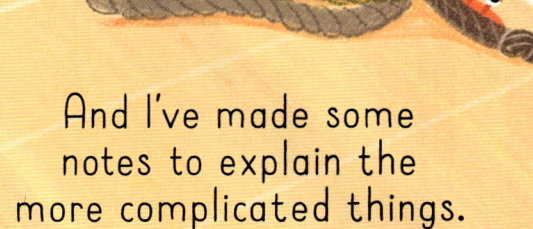

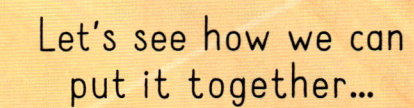

And I've made some notes to explain the more complicated things.

Let's see how we can put it together...

People are putting lots of yucky things into the sea...
It stinks!
...and taking out TOO many fish.
Yikes!
Sea creatures, plants and algae are in danger...
There's too much CO_2.
Our shells are dissolving.
...and that's bad for us, too.
We all need the OXYGEN plants make.
Climate change is a BIG PROBLEM.
HELP! My house is flooding!
But we can all be part of the solution.
Then we'll make much less CO_2.
Burn LESS
coal
oil
gas

The people in charge need to DO MORE.

GOVERNMENTS take action!

Make companies pay for their pollution.

Countries need to make strict LAWS and ENFORCE them.

BAN OVERFISHING

BAN throwaway plastic

We can ALL play our part by making ocean-friendly choices...

"I've changed my speedboat to a kayak."

"Paddleboarding is so peaceful!"

helping to RESTORE NATURE...

"We're planting more mangrove trees."

making less litter...

"We're stopping litter from reaching the sea."

DON'T DROP IT, BIN IT!

...and telling everyone about our AMAZING ocean.

"Thank you for watching!"

Our schools might show the video in assembly.

This was made by one of our students.

OUR MOVIE
HELP the DOLPHINS

It could go VIRAL...

Have you seen this?!

...and inspire lots of campaigners.

We all need the OXYGEN plants make.

Plastic WON'T rot away.

BAN throwaway plastic

This shouldn't be allowed.

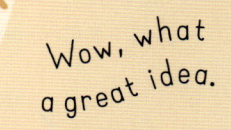

STOP SEWAGE SPLURGES

Wow, what a great idea.

SAVE THE DOLPHINS

Our government will have to sit up and take notice.

SEWAGE DISCHARGE

Oh dear, it's true. Water companies have been discharging more raw sewage.

We must introduce stricter laws and fines.

THERE'S A SWIRLING SOUP OF PLASTIC IN THE OCEAN THAT'S **THREE TIMES** THE SIZE OF FRANCE

And countries around the world could agree to help the ocean.

The world NEEDS action! Let's have a global treaty on STOPPING plastic pollution.

WORLD LEADERS' OCEAN MEETING

We'll sign it!

So will we.

And us!

Us too.

183

Woof!

We really CAN help the dolphins.

And all kinds of sea creatures.

And you'll be helping the rest of the planet too.

Including humans!

Hurrah!

THANK YOU!

Goodbye.

It was wonderful to meet you.

Take care.

Good luck.

Goodbye, and thanks for all your help!

Enjoy the rest of your summer.

What next?

The problems the dolphins and their friends describe in this story are REAL and affect us ALL. But the GOOD NEWS is that things are already changing...

PROTECTED AREAS of our SEAS and OCEANS

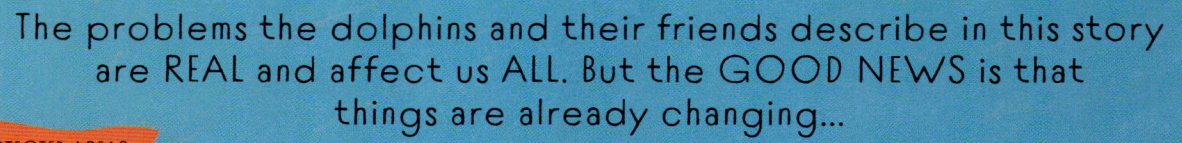

Large parts of the ocean have become PROTECTED AREAS, with restrictions on shipping and fishing.

Governments responsible for 40% of the world's coastlines have promised to END OVERFISHING and help fish populations to recover.

Thank you!

Many countries have already BANNED single-use plastic items and are introducing a TAX on plastic packaging.

Areas equivalent to thousands of football fields have been successfully replanted with seagrass, and many more restoration projects are planned.

Thanks!

There's still LOTS MORE TO DO and we can all play a part in protecting our oceans.

I'm going to be an INVENTOR and develop a natural alternative to plastic.

I'm going to be a MARINE BIOLOGIST and learn more about how we can protect dolphins.

I'm going to be a POLITICIAN and make laws stopping companies from causing pollution.

I'm going to start a CONSERVATION CHARITY, raising money to restore coastal areas.

Coastal Conservation
$1,000,000

I'm going to make CAMPAIGN VIDEOS and help people understand what's really going on.

I'm going to be a TEACHER and explain the facts about climate change and protecting our planet.

GLOSSARY

Here are some of the important words in these stories, and what they mean.

acidic – sour or sharp-tasting.

air conditioning unit – an electric device used to take heat out of rooms and cool them down.

Arctic – the area around the North pole, at the northern-most point of planet Earth.

battery – a container for storing electricity.

boreal forests – a vast band of forests stretching across the chilly north.

carbon – one of the important chemical elements that all things in the universe are made from.

carbon dioxide (CO_2) – one of the heat-trapping gases people make when they burn fossil fuels.

cattle – a group of cows or bulls or a mixture of both.

chemicals – substances made using a scientific process. There are chemicals in nature, but the ones causing pollution in this book are made by people.

clean energy – energy made without giving off nasty gases.

climate change – a change in weather patterns around the world. Human activities are making the world get warmer, and this is causing climate change.

compost – a rich kind of soil made from food and garden waste.

coral reef – a large underwater structure made by thousands of tiny animals called coral polyps.

crops – plants farmers grow.

discharge – letting out a waste liquid or gas.

electric vehicle – a vehicle that runs off electricity, stored inside a battery.

electricity – a way of getting energy from one place to another. Lots of things we use today need electricity to work.

food chain – living things lined up in the order of who eats what.

food web – how lots of food chains link together.

fossil fuels – coal, oil and natural gas.

fumes – dirty gases puffed out by vehicles or chimneys.

green bridge – a bridge planted with local trees and other plants, to make a safe crossing for wildlife.

greenhouse gas – a gas which traps in heat when it's added to the air.

hive – a box shape built by humans to keep honeybees in.

insulation – a layer of padding to keep out the cold.

landslide – when a large area of land slips away.

mangrove – a type of tree that lives in salty water along warm coastlines.

methane – a greenhouse gas made when things rot underground or by cows and sheep burping.

microplastics – very small pieces of plastic. Plastic litter breaks up into microplastics.

nectar – the sweet liquid a plant makes to attract insects.

organic – grown without using chemical sprays.

overfishing – taking too many fish from the ocean, so whole species start to die out.

oxygen – the gas we all need to breathe in to live, and another important chemical element in the universe.

particles – tiny pieces of something.

pest – an insect or other animal that damages crops.

plankton – very small living things that float in the sea.

plantation – a large farm where just one type of crop is grown.

pollen – a fine powder found on or inside flowers.

pollination – when pollen from one flower reaches another flower. This needs to happen so the plant can make seeds.

pollinator – an insect or other animal that spreads pollen from one flower to another.

pollution – harmful stuff that damages the planet.

power station – a factory that makes electricity.

pulp – a soft, wet mush.

rainforest – a lush, dense forest that's rich in wildlife.

rewilding – restoring an area to its natural state.

sewage – liquid and solid waste from toilets.

solar panel – a flat surface that can turn the sun's energy into electricty.

soy beans – a type of bean, rich in protein. They grow in pods, like peas. They can be used in animal food, or to feed humans directly.

species – a group of the same kind of living things. For example, scarlet macaws are a species of bird.

sustainable – using something in a way that doesn't damage it or ruin it for the future.

steam engine – an invention that uses the power of steam to make things move.

treaty – a written agreement between two or more countries, signed by their leaders.

wildflowers – any flowers that grow naturally in the wild. They can be planted in all kinds of places.

wind turbine – a tall pole with spinning blades that makes electricity from the wind.

Books and trees

Usborne books are made from a mixture of recycled paper, and wood pulp from sustainable, well-managed forests. The FSC symbol on the back of our books show that the paper has been responsibly sourced. Usborne is also supporting reforestation projects with our partners at Ecologi.

Edited by Jane Chisholm
Climate change expert: Dr. Steve Smith
Pollination & biodiversity expert: Professor Jeff Ollerton
Trees expert: Dr. Manuel Luján
Ocean expert: Jo Ruxton

With thanks to Zoe Wray and Holly Lamont

First published in 2023 by Usborne Publishing Limited, 83-85 Saffron Hill, London, EC1N 8RT. usborne.com Copyright © 2023, 2022, 2021 Usborne Publishing Limited. The name Usborne and the Balloon logo are trade marks of Usborne Publishing Limited. All rights reserved. No part of this publication may be reproduced, stored in a retrieval system or transmitted in any form or by any means without the prior permission of the publisher. UE.

Children should be supervised online. Please follow the internet safety guidelines at Usborne Quicklinks. Usborne Publishing is not responsible and does not accept liability for the availability or content of any website other than its own, or for any exposure to harmful, offensive or inaccurate material which may appear on the Web.